AMERICAN REAL

Published by

Copyright © M Wayne
Enterprises   2013

All rights reserved. Except as
permitted under the U.S. Copyright Act
of 1976, no part of this publication
may be reproduced, distributed, or
transmitted in any form or by any
means, or stored in a database or
retrieval system without the prior
written permission of the publisher.

For my mother, without whose blessing some of these words would have taken a lifetime and some would have never been written…

For my professors, Neil, Kate and Trista, whose impact is very real and not yet fully understood…

And for my friends, who have taught me that family can be chosen; that I am not alone; that there are others like me;

that I am not defined by anything other than what I am today; that have helped me succeed; that have soaked my shirts with their tears; that have allowed my tears to soak their shirts; that have fed me; that have given me so much there are not enough words or enough pages to describe…

I love you all, and these words are meant for you.

American Real

Prelude	9
53..................	Holidays
Love	59
67..................	God
Family	71
97..................	Friendship
Self	111
131................	Country
Matters of Importance	139

Prelude to American Real

Melting

For Christ's sake someone please,
stop pouring the water
she's melting.
and I don't want to watch anymore.

It wouldn't be so bad,
not so bad at all
if it all came at once
 it there was just one fall.
but a little at a time?
and I stare at the wall.

Melting, God, melting away
and I still hear the call.

There's nothing I can do to stop it
and no mercy in the pour
I want this to hurt a little less
I hold parts of her off the floor
I put them back and they just fall down
I can't do this anymore.

Melting, God, melting away
lost now is the lore.

Maybe this wouldn't be so bad
if I hadn't seen it twice
maybe the truth is that I AM
isn't always so nice
but just a little mercy, just this once
watching comes at a high price.

Melting, God melting away
just like winter's ice.

Father, please, show some mercy!
You took the viola this way!
must life be without music?
I can barely hear the piano play
I want to hear it just a little longer
please God, take her not away.

But melting, God still melting
a little more today
I watch, but I can't see
my mother's face today.

Calling

The boy called me just today
tried to call himself a man
though in the mirror he's still cloudy
nowhere as clear as I think he can.
I told him all I know this time
he chose the noise over the plan.
Though I know how much it took for me
for him, I don't understand.

I wanted to show him to life
to teach him about the pain
to care for him in my arms
to shelter him from rain
he chose the madness from the light
he thinks they are the same.
Though I know how much it took for me
for him, it must seem insane.

A child cannot see to safely cross
lest they hold their Father's hand
It's the same as we grow old
we are lions held by the lamb
lost in the unending sea
a compass leads us to land.
Though I know what it took for me
for him, he must break to bend.

I hope soon he will see as I
for that, he'll have to break
I had to go blind to see the light
to sleep so I could wake
and only in the Truth could I find myself
for Truth you cannot fake.
Though I know what it took for me
for him I pray less, for his sake.

A Friend Lost

All he wants to do is kill
he's forgotten how to live
and when I see behind his eyes
I know the death is his
I wish my friend would come awake
far gone, sleep causes this.

I want him to know as I know
I die almost every day.
All knowledge comes at a cost
seems interest is what I pay
and knowing what I know now
I had to learn to pray

not for the things I've done
nor for what I wish to be
not for the future or the past
but for what my eyes now see.
I pray for what I hold deep inside
I pray I'm never set free.

I hope, my friend, you understand

I wish you no ill will

but as you look out the window

know that it's different

from inside the sill

and there are other ways to learn to live

than to learn how to kill.

Wildflowers

I came here to find
along with peace and serenity
to ease a troubled mind
and when I got to where they were last week
I found that they had died.

I wanted to see them so much today
as they remind me of my friend
the kindness she always sends my way
kindness, it seems, she'll always lend
and it seems right that they have died
short their season, quick their end.

It's hard now to explain it
the Truth I found on trail
if everything were not just so
if not right as the mail
I would've never seen them a week ago
for in Truth, they are so frail.

And I thought, how funny that is
how strong I thought they were
It amazes me
that anything would grow next to that dead fir
with soil loose on the side of Cheyenne Mountain
it seems nothing is for sure.

All of that is true
and the Truth I can finally see
wildflowers don't grow where I want them to
they grow where they're supposed to be.
Then I remembered how beautiful they were
on the mountain, bold and free
and I realized I too am a wildflower
though of Virginia they reminded me.

Here I Am

Empty, I Am... I guess,
Is how I need to be
Empty, So that,
I can just see me
And it fills me with joy,
To see it so free...

And I say,

        Here I Am,
        Here am I.

I get lost in the woods,
Which is why I go there
With my soul running on empty,
And vacant, my stare
I drive it like I stole it,
And it hardly seems fair

And I say,

        Here I Am,
        Here am I.

As I climb to the top,

Thick are my tears

Lost in so many places,

For so many years

What took me so long,

To realize my fears?

And I say,

                Here I Am,

                Here am I.

There on that trail,

Screaming at the sky

I was humbled by beauty,

So much I did cry

And when I got to The Rock,

I sat down, finally died,

Saying, "Here I Am, here am I."

Hunger

When you called yesterday,
I hungry, empty and weak
so broken down and tired
it was so hard to speak
I haven't eaten that much
it seems, this last week.

And you asked,
"Is there anything I can do?"

I wanted to say, "Yeah,
how 'bout some chicken and rice?!"
but I was lost in my mind
so I knew to think twice
and when I told you, "no."
I knew you weren't just being nice.

When you asked,
"Is there anything I can do?"

You sighed for a moment
there was a long pause
and I could tell you were hurt
in that moment because
you knew I was empty
you know what hunger does.

When you asked,
"Is there anything I can do?"

The last week's not been good
less than 800 calories a day
and when Dad looked in my eyes
he didn't know what to say
but each day he served me three meals
and at each one we'd pray.

And you asked,
"Is there anything I can do?"

It seems so odd
as I've been here before
and though I'm pretty far down

I'm not on the floor
I know the door will be opened
when I knock on the door.

And you asked,
"Is there anything I can do?"

Then you said to, "imagine
getting a hug from me."
and that I did
and in that moment I felt free
your kindness touched my heart
and I started to weep.

When you asked,
"Is there anything I can do?"

Now that I can think
there is just one thing
that you could do for me
that your kindness could bring
a gift so simple
carried on your wing.

Should you ask,
"Is there anything I can do?"

I would ask that you please
do not worry for me
for if seeing me like this hurts you
then I don't want you to see
and if I know you're okay
somehow, it sets me free.
Have faith in the Father
and what He wills to be.
In faith, darlin' please,
don't worry for me.

The Education of a Wandering Man

It's been a hard day
hard to know what to do
hard to realize the Truth
hard to learn something I knew
and what I Am learning
is not what I wanted to.

In the education of a wandering man.

What I have found
is not the treasure I seek
it seems backward from Truth
the world inherits the meek
what I once thought was strong
I now see as weak.

In the education of a wandering man.

It seems all I do
is under attack
it doesn't matter the wall
how high the bricks stack
the one Truth I have found?
you've gotta watch your back.

In the education of a wandering man.

It's a one lane road
which is way to damn long
there is no music
unless you sing the song
and what seems right to you
to the world, is so wrong.

In the education of a wandering man.

The things that I thought were
are no longer real
the ante is high
and I got a bad deal
the hope I once had
I can no longer feel.

In the education of a wandering man.

It would be nice to have someone
just some company
to walk along side
who could also see
that nothing seems to come
and nothing comes free.

In the education of a wandering man.

Volunteers

People who've not been hungry
shouldn't read what I write today
it may make you awkward and uncomfortable
in an unfamiliar way
so with caution please proceed
to what happened yesterday.

For you are just like me (as am I)

I went down to the bank
to fill boxes with grain
fruit, vegetables and all the like
and all of it the same
I found comfort in humanity
for they were all in pain.

Just like me (as am I)

It was hard to work around the food
when I have not eaten much
hunger can drive a man insane
the smell, the taste and such
although hard to work around it
They were grateful for a human touch.

Just like me (as am I)

When I saw the look in the first man's eye
and broken, he was too
I could see clear wrong from right
amazing what pain gives to you
he, as I, glad to see a smile on my face
and I could tell he saw straight through.

Just like me (as am I)

When his box full, he looked at me
misty eyed, "thank you. God bless."
"You too," I said. My eyes wet too
and it was tight in my chest
with pride far gone, no right from wrong
he was stronger than that, I guess.

Just like me (as am I)

As I walked out the door, pride on the floor
with my own box in my hands
with tears in my eyes, I knew not to cry
I was grateful I could still stand.
I'll remember him long, with his pride far gone
and without, he the better man.

Just like me (as am I)

Walkin' with a Boy

My God the alarm was early today
but then that was his choice.
Seems a child listens better
when there is consistency in your voice
even so, I wish it weren't raining,
my socks are getting moist.

Walkin' with a boy
makin' me a man.

We are up here on top of the world
and yet, still so very small
seems a child has a lot of growing to do
regardless of how tall
what I must do to build him up
is to tear down a wall.

Walkin' with a boy
makin' me a man.

And although a child is learning
somedays it's hard to teach
I'm trying to remember how a child
is always in The Father's reach.
Although I want him to know it all
I must learn not to preach.

Walkin' with a boy
makin' me a man.

And I promise, Father, to do my best
as I learned, the best I can
to listen for the Viola playing
from heaven where I stand
And always remember who I Am
walkin' with a boy
makin' me a man.

Unheard

People cannot hear me speak
Don't know why, seems it's true
I open my mouth, words come out
but no one hears them though
sometimes even I can't hear me
though I can always hear you.

Like whispering into the dark
I can't hear within
I don't know why my words are lost here
somewhere in the din
doesn't matter how I speak them
some days I can't win.

My own father can't hear me
he too lost within his words
unable to listen to his own son
in his ears are his own words
he has chosen the path for himself
a path, I think, is for the birds.

My mother cannot hear me
for she can't hear through the dark
though she's been not listening for years
the contrast is now stark
she wants to tell me all about the trees
when she can't see the bark.

My best friend doesn't listen
though it's not entirely his fault
his life is running down the road
so far now from the melt
funny how he knows so much
but can't tell the pepper from the salt.

The preacher doesn't listen
for he wants to hear the Truth
but I can't believe he could hear one word
as a sayer of so much soothe
funny how a man can bark so loud
when he has not one tooth.

The child doesn't listen
children seldom do
they cannot listen, but THEY MUST BE HEARD!
because they know it better than you
though they haven't lived nearly long enough
to see it through.

I don't think God is listening
that's hard for me to say
once upon a time, I found comfort
in kneeling down to pray
but my Father left his Son alone
and I cannot feel today.

A Light in the Attic

The attic, a place I wonder
seldom do I roam
always somewhere deep inside
never far from home
the darkness that lingers there
feels like my tomb.

The attic, a place I remember
that I came to dread
never go there too long
the hunger must be fed
always fearful, watchful, careful eyes
would rather leave instead.

The Attic,
My childhood ripped
out from under somewhere up there
the darkness dwelling in that space
the black, unending stare
the hate of things just for being
the will without the care.

The Attic,
so long avoided
I forgot the things left inside
a small stuffed dog down in a box
where once I tried to hide
the cat that tried to keep me safe
when there was no one left to confide.

The Attic,
with my comic books and Gramma's watch
hidden somewhere in the mess
been so long since I read Superman
I remember less, and less
my gray and green army guys
who kept me safe there in the nest.

The Attic,
shocked to see
is where I was today
when Shell's words rang in my mind
and a boy began to play
an old book fell on the floor
opening in a peculiar way.

And there was a light on
in The Attic
I remember mom reading to me
Gramma's watch tickin' loud
my army guys runnin' free
I was thinkin' bout Superman
what could he see?

A light on in The Attic
with my puppy out of the box
Ted the cat, standing guard at my feet
keepin' me safe from life's hard knocks
here I am lookin' at my feet
in my favorite pair of socks.

In The Attic,
with the light on
really ain't so bad
as I look round in the boxes
there's a whole bunch I forgot I had.

I think I'll stay round here a while
see what makes this thing tick
remember the things that made me happy
forget some stuff that made me sick
It's nice to be here for a change
with a light in The Attic.

Behind the Curtain

I should be writing this in the other book,
the one that ties shut
somehow I cannot dig it out
but then, I suppose, it's already cut
I wish there were an easier way
I wish for a lot of things... but,

There are three who come to eat here
Three who come to pray
Three who hate their mother
Three who wish not to stay
astonishing that I forgot to see
Three are here today.

Awake here in this valley
'cause it's where I learned to fight
where I learned to stretch my legs
where I learned it right
and fuck all them in my own way
Fuck 'em all with all my might.

Three who came to kill here
Three who came for death
Three who wish to taste blood
Three who can taste fear on their breath
astonishing , I forgot to see
Three, and one wants meth.

No sleep here in this valley
Damn Kids hear anyway
fuckin' things won't shut up
whining all the damned way
always cryin' all the time
even when it's okay.

Three who came to die here
Three who die here all the time
Three who beg for silence
Three who wish for mine
I can't believe you forgot us
somewhere in the rhyme.

No rest in this valley
no rest will we ever find
our makers made us what we are
and that's what keeps us blind
there ain't no more like us
no more of our kind.

Three who came together
one who wishes to go
Three who don't understand that
one who wants them to know
Three who don't want to listen
one who wants them to grow
Three who know no forgiveness
one who prays it will show.

Dirty South

In the Dirty South
where the truth is a lie
they smile to your face
then beat you till you cry
everyone knows deep inside
and holds to their alibi.

They hide behind manners
the people out here
they control you with them
that, and some fear
in a moment of truth
I can now see so clear.

The opressed hide in their anger
wear it all over their face
so they too cannot see
how to live in this place
blinded with rage
even to the human race.

The people out here
not quite what they seem
they've been fighting so long
they forgot what it means
to live by love
wash your heart clean

Funny how I couldn't see it
'til I came face to face
saw the pain in their eyes
hear another disgrace
livin' by the sword
dyin' by the race.

In the company of "gentle-"men
I heard them vomit out their hate
speaking so much disgust
even I cannot create
puking so politely
no one did debate.

Just two days later
as I walked through the mall
smiling at one of beauty and color
a kind gesture, as I strolled down the hall
the rage from his eyes
though justified, said it all.

This has gone on too long
yet still un-done
an inheritance of sin
from father to son
a battle fought, we've forgotten
why we'd even begun.

Another Bitch in the Wall

She says,

I chew to loud

eat too much

do not chew my food enough.

That I'm lazy, fat, a pig

a slob and

I deserve the way she treats me.

She will never trust me for trust is earned

for that matter, so is respect.

That my writing's shit

the comma's wrong

and because she loves me, I should change that.

Her ex-husband is right

even when he was wrong

and he can work circles around me.

That she knows best

like she has all along

and the problem?

      the problem, is me.
That I'm lazy, fat, a slob, a pig
and I deserve the way she treats me.
If I don't like it, well
I can just leave
she doesn't have to take my shit.

I'm lazy, fat, a slob, a pig
that's just how she puts it.

That addicts are somehow cured by God
and she knows because she's never been one
and she can't quit smoking
for even two weeks when her children challenge her to.

That she tries the hardest and does the most
and anyone could see that
because she missed my birthday
put me down on Thanksgiving
because she didn't want to do that.

That I'm lazy, fat, a slob, a pig
and how could I not see it.

I was blinded, I guess, by my 4.0 that I held for one year of college.
by my instructor's praise
and the scholarship I was nominated for this year.
by the 17 credits I pulled last term with a part time job and a marriage class and the kids.
and even with that, it's still 3.92
She gets on me and can kiss my ass.

In the still of the night
moon held on high
the silence comes over the din
she tells me she loves me
more than anyone else
if she didn't, she wouldn't say anything
I leave the bed, her words
behind.
Because to sleep, I must be
free of them.

American Real

I hate these words. They come from a terrible place and I am not given the freedom to choose. I have to write them. They're stuck inside me and if I don't write them, if I refuse: I break. I fall down like a soldier on his sword. It's like reliving suicide, the worst possible part, where you lose the struggle with the gun in your mouth, the trigger pulled, the hammer falls and its over. But its never over. When the gun is fired and my blood is all over the paper, I wake. And there is more. There is always more. I live in the moment of the falling hammer. I do not write these words because I like them, I write them because I have to. My muse like a southern slave owner who hates what I am for the fear of it.

I wish I didn't have to write them. But the gun is always in my mouth, the whip always on my back. It is an awful thing to be a writer.

I have to go now, the words are coming.

Holidays

Wednesday

Today is
Wednesday
nothing more
nothing less
hump-day
middle of the week
my weekend
my birthday
Wednesday
and I'm tired of it already.

I celebrated with
Ex#1, Ex#2 and
I don't care to
anymore.

These "days"
they come
and
they go
with little care for
what they mean.

Wednesday
the hardest day of the fucking week
to spell
and I am tired of spelling
this day
this week
life.

And my friends are growing
thin, with so few
having so little
interest in
the who of
what I am
and the what of
how I have to be.

Mom called and
sung happy birthday
to the answering machine
she likes it
makes her feel like
my mom
that thing she never was for me.

How many Wednesdays more must
I endure before the lights go dim?
Before I am put out
to see the infinite Thursday
that must come after
the long Wednesday?

Some moral code must hold me
fast to what is
has never been
cannot be
for me.

It's a social contract:

smile.

thank you.

of course I'm happy.

doing well.

so that they feel better

so that they feel normal.

But I didn't sign this contract

and

I don't think it was written

for me.

Wednesday beatings

rapings

why not? It's Wednesday after all!

and after the first 15 years

what should I expect on Wednesday?

another beating?

cake?

Make new Wednesdays they say
friends
shrinks
people who've never had 15 years
of Wednesdays.
And when I try on their hats
I can't find my shoes.
So I see my Wednesdays for what they are:
Wednesdays.
The hardest fucking day of the week to spell.
No contracts.
No bullshit.
The day to wish for Thursday.

Love

Crashing

Broken hearts mend slow,
and words that were kept,
spoken. Gently rested
upon the ears of her
beautiful. He cannot imagine
any other
way.

They touch, gentle as words in a place
where time holds gently those two who
are not allowed to breathe. She does not
run and he is careful. So careful not to break
the one who he is now broken for... not broken
by.

Lips hold a careful breeze between best friends
while frogs chatter and rain falls upon their faces with
fingers laced together. Risking a moment for a moment
more, they linger... and the night goes on.

There is no place to say what becomes of the broken
few who know this dance. Caution weighing heavy where
the danger becomes worth the risk to a heart broken that
no longer wishes to bend, and would rather
become broken anew.

How to Write a Love Poem

1.
Asking me to do this,
Is like tearing the wallet from
the pauper's hands, to make him pay
for the orphanage.
2.
It did not exist at home
unless taped to the shafts of switches
I learned to murder before smile
and my father creating me
broken, wounded, brittle.
Left with mother
I learned to
SILENCE
lightly,
danger ahead.

3.

So this is how it's done,

I start with my fingers, pressing them

evenly upon my breastbone, harder, until

my fingernails pierce my chest and I begin

to bleed. Push past the

fat and soft flesh, where I begin

to hit, knuckle to bone.

Hit harder.

Harder still!

Until the crunching bone breaks

and my chest is exposed to air. Insert

my fingers between and pull

ribs broken, screaming to protect

the brittle, hardened flesh beating

within.

Tear it, slurping from inside and lay
it on the floor before me, surround it with paper,
I kneel,
Raise my fists
and pound the flesh to begin
to soften, to make right the unknown tenderness.
Drops of crimson splattering
the poem.

this is what I do
and today I am not in love.

Unmade

Butterflied stomach
I wait.
Clicking white keys
reminds me of her with
no reason for
their memory
but
the strands of
her hair woven
in my fingers
and my mind.

And there is something I want her to know:

You do not have to love me.

Because you are
beautiful,
not just your Michelangelo curves,
gentle brown eyes, or
soft tender lips.
Your beauty

goes down

to the bone. Tucked

in between the sinew and marrow

it resides

and I do not wish

that you should change.

For I would never hope

to cage what you are

to become something I made.

No man could make you

and your beauty lies there

and I am the same

no woman could create what I am.

But if you feel as I do

I wish you would walk

with me a while

if only to see where the path leads together

God

Hey God,

Came to your house
today, snubbed by the man at the door. Scars
on my arms, scars you gave
me, scars
I can't help but wear.

Sat down like the rest and
listened. Same old shit. Nineveh
and a fucking whale. Nineveh
covered in puke on the shore.
Nineveh, Nineveh, Nineveh.
And The Asshole that sent
me? Nowhere to be found.

Shake the hand of the woman
behind, loves me, doesn't know me, doesn't
want to. I come here
for peace, so tired of hiding behind
words, from in-between syllables

I peek out to the world that

hates my eyes. I can't hide

them anymore they sneak

out from behind consonants, screaming

to be seen, needing the sun.

I hate them

I hate You

I hate me

standing here in Nineveh. I long

for the desert. So much easier to be

alone under the shade

of that tree. In a place where

I'm not allowed to be

who I Am

for the fear of it,

mine

theirs

ours

Yours.

Family

Killing Felons

Murder came easy
for me. Did it you Dear
brother? Do you fear Dear
brother? Fear not, Dear brother,
your sins are safe
from These words.
To-day I will tell
me.

I was 12 when I began
killing innocence, innocently
and became the monster my mother tried not
to let me see.
Our father's switch
I was
violence
I was
terrible
I was
murderer, innocent, our family history
I was. And some days
still am.

I restrain myself
daily.
Hold back what lingers violently on the tips
of my fists to keep it from becoming the thing that it was
that I was
that I am.

And my friend tells me
she doesn't see it. That I
am like a big teddy bear, and I smile
to conceal my shame,
put my blue eyes to the floor
to hide the eyes of those
who I have made to fear
my hands, our family history,
our father's switch. That I
struggle so desperately to un-become.

But even with that, Dear
brother, you know
that were you here, Dear
brother to see my eyes to-day? Oh, Dear
brother you would see them
no more.

Because I have heard of
your daughter's cries, dried your
son's tears, both of them and YOU
GREY HAIR, YOU ARE NOT ASHAMED...
but I can smell you, even from 3,000 miles
away, I can smell you, and you stink of our father
you reek of our mother, and the putrid smell of our family
history <u>begs the wind not blow</u>, lest I should smell it, and come
for you, and all that you are, you motherfucker, and all you pass down,
you sonofabitch, and what you and your cunt of a fucking wife have done
makes me want... soo bad...

not to hide

my eyes

from

you.

but

I

do

I do, I do, I do. Though some

days, like to-

day I do

not

know

why.

Un-Common Table

Thanks-giving
and a man walks from the ice.
I greet him
seat him and he pulls from his empty pocket,
wooden nickel.

To pay for a meal
he cannot afford,
to miss

I put the wood grained meal
back in his leathered hand.
"you don't need this to-day"
"no one will charge you to-day"
"today you can just
eat"

Bring him
moist turkey
cranberry sauce
home-made stuffing, green beans, yams, mashed potatoes
and gravy.

And Water

And Coffee.

and he eats
morsels of flavor explode between teeth
against gums, tart puckers lips in a mouth full of
empty for too long.

and he drinks
each swallow oasised
washing sour-tart
cleansing the sweet salt and fat.

his Plate Empty
I ask,
"would you like some more?"
His eyes plead me

"I do",
he says, "but
it's just that
it's been a while since I..."
he sighs and his eyes are suddenly mine
tired, humble,
not wanting to
burden another with a dark secret

"don't worry" they said
"I'm okay" they said
"I can do this" they said

and I know the shame of hunger,
the filth of poverty
so I raise my hand
to stop his speech
"it's okay bro... I've been there"

His shoulders rest
eyes stop pleading
and his jaw unclenches
from a secret we bear together

And I smile
to hide my watering eyes
and he smiles
to hide our dirty hunger
our filthy poverty
with his strong back
small stomach
pocket full of
wooden nickel
and black coffee.

Ode To My Mother

Do you remember Ma?
Remember when you were young and in love
when you met my father
and you were happy?
Do you remember
when you cut the cake on your wedding day
and everything seemed like it would be perfect?
Do you remember that Ma?
Cause I don't.

Do you remember Ma?
When Dad walked down the steps,
put his ring on the desk
Leaving a note that said
"I'm sorry."
A note I couldn't fuckin read Ma
and the whole world fell apart
and He looked at me with almost a tear in his eye and said
"I'm sorry, Son."
walked out the door.
Do you remember, Ma?
Cause I do.

And do you remember Ma?
When you bounced us from relative to relative to
relative to family friend because
You lost your fucking crackers and
didn't know what to do.
Do you remember that, Ma?
When we lived with Ellen,
Grandma and Grandpa
everywhere but home, Ma
and you decided I needed a father figure
so you sent me to "Bud"
a "friend" of the family
and after the first visit
I didn't wanna go back and I
stood at the top of the stairs crying,
begging not to go and him standing there
watching me beg and you asked me
"Why?"
and me begging not to go and you asked
"Why?"
and I couldn't tell you Ma?
so you sent me anyway Ma?
cause I couldn't tell you Ma?

He raped me that night Ma.
Do you remember Ma?
Can you fucking remember Ma?
He raped me Ma
I couldn't make him stop Ma
Where were you Ma?
Why did you send me there Ma?
Why didn't you listen to me Ma?
I didn't want to go back Ma
I didn't want to go Ma
Do you remember Ma?
I do. And I can't ever not go back again.

And do you remember Ma?
When you sent us
to live with our dad
and he put a cigar out on my arm
broke a board over my ass
Do you remember,
Do you remember,
him passing out
unconscious with a needle in his arm Ma
do you remember him beating us to within

inches of our lives, Ma
Do you remember any of that shit
Ma? No...
I do. I can't forget it.

Do you remember Ma?
Remember those moments when we came back
when I really started to fight
every day a battle at school
and you thought that I was
the bad kid?
Do you remember Ma?
Remember when my teacher was
dragging me downstairs
because of a fight I'd been in
and you didn't want to hear the reason why
I hit that Motherfucker and
walked myself to the principle's office
you beat the shit out of me
for a half hour
Remember Ma?
The principle said
"You were wrong." Ma

The principle said "I
was right." Ma
that teacher nearly got fired Ma
but it was my fault because
I was in the fourth grade
I was my father's son.
Remember?

And lets not forget
the rest of the fourth grade because
that's when you let me smoke weed, Ma
when my uncle gave it to me, Ma
with your permission, Ma
I smoked weed
at nine years old
a little young don't you think, Ma
what do you think, Ma
what do you see to-day, Ma
and there I am fighting, Ma
and my uncle who gave me the joint
Is telling you
"Schools are institutions
Schools are institutions

Schools are institutions!"
and he's choking you
in the living room
and I run outside and
I get my bat
and I walk back in
and five, ten of my friends
and the fucking neighbors
they all hold me
hold me back
Do you remember, Ma?
he was choking the life
out of you
in the motherfucking living room
and my friends are holding me
back.
They're all holding me back

And do you remember what you
told me after?
That they were right
that I would have just gotten hurt
Do you remember that, Ma?

You were wrong, Ma.
You were dead wrong
cause if it took ten motherfuckers
to hold me back
that one piece of shit didn't
stand a goddamned chance.
and it took over a month
for the bruises on your neck
to heal.

And do you remember, Ma?
Remember that same year
I started selling drugs
making my own money
at nine years old
I was that kid
they warned you about
that kid on the playground
in the after school specials.
Do you remember
can you remember
remember
remember, Ma?

Remember as I got older, Ma?
Remember when
I had charges hangin over my head
and lawyers coming to see you for
what I had done
and we're going to specialists
to find out what's
wrong with your boy
as if you weren't there?
And I can't remember
and we're going to
all these appointments
seein all these doctors
takin a million tests
where they tell me
"It's okay, Son.
Be honest"
Remember
remember what they told you
what they told you about your boy
how he was
"Going to prison
Going to murder someone

by the time he was 15"

how he was

"Going to spend his

life in prison

he can't be fixed

we don't know what happened

he's fucked up

he's going to do bad things

and

this is the next serial killer"

And do you remember?

Remember what you said

To them, Ma?

You looked him straight in the eye

and said,

"No

my son

can do better

than this.

You don't know

him

like I do"

Remember, Ma

that one time

in my whole fucking childhood

when you were right?

Do you remember, Ma?

A couple years ago

when I split up with

ex #2

and I'm livin in a trailer

in my friends yard

and you called me up

on my cell

in between my classes

as an honor roll student in college

and in between my job

where I was barely making

enough to eat

do remember what you called

me and said?

You said

"Son

you are a writer Son

and you do what you have to do,

Son.

And I want you to know something

Son,

You Don't Be Afraid To Write Me.

You can write me ugly,

Son.

As ugly as I was,

Son.

Tell me horrible,

Son."

Do you remember, Ma?

Remember what you said?

"Don't worry about how

I'll look,

Son.

You have to do this,

Son.

This is important

Son.

And if I'm gonna look bad,

because I know I will, I'll deal with

that,

Son.

That's my job,
Son.
It's okay, I can take it."

Do remember
remember that time ma?
The day you gave your Son permission
to be
to write
to become
to tell
to truth
Cause I'll never forget.

Handful

His mother warns: a handful will kill. The nine-year old listens,
to remember, to make it stop. He stands,
from the sofa, like a soldier, head bowed,
battle over, pulls red, white packages.

Tylenol, two in each; the nine-year old measures:
the counter brown, the bowl white, empty packages, himself,
a glass of water, a hand-full, white and red. Swallows:
capsules, like bullets loading: click, click, click. Coldwater sneaks
past trembling lips, wanting gums, willing throat and with trigger pulled,
the nothing comes: tick tock, tick tock, tick tock.

Blue eyes thrust awake, to dark, to drooled carpet, wet cheek and
tongue dry. Brain pounding against his skull, keeping perfect rhythm
with his heart. He stands, unwilling warrior, shoulders fallen, gun jammed
unnoticed.
The boy, a man now, red beard thick, like a soldier
shoulders tall, un-proud, blue eyes stare distant, knowing.
A woman:
younger than he, brown eyes pleading, thrusts her hand out for his like a child
her hand weathered, torn-soft: like his, he takes it. A handful.

The Importance of Animals

First there was Jake.
Big yellow dog
who gave us freedom from
bears, cougars
Dad
and allowed us to sit in
the old growth where
the trees spoke
peace, quiet child
broken forest
that Dad relentlessly cut down.
He was a logger.

Ted.
Tabby tom cat
watched me while I
slept and
made sure I had food
sleeping on my chest.

Midnight.
My first dog black

with white paws, chest
and chin, she
protected me from
burglars, friends
Mom and
brought me sleep
showed me safety
with eyes closed.

Mya.
Blue merle Aussie Sheppard, she
stops flashbacks (I don't know how)
my friend
licks my tears clean
my best
friend
listens to the night
so I don't have to
lets me to
sleep
rest
peace.

Friendship

Friends

Friendship,
handed around the room
like a pot of coffee after church
add sugar to make it sweeter
cream to smooth over the bitter
drink it until you feel better
then pour what's left down the sink

But my friends
aren't the kind you find in the after church coffee hour.
Though some do go
not because they are holy or righteous,
but because they know
they are not.

Drug dealers and addicts
homeless and rank
they are gritty, mean, arrogant
hungry, bitter motherfuckers
who carry guns, smoke crack
and speak exactly what is on their mind.
They are tattooed, pierced

overweight, gangly
convicted felons, former murderers
and celibate pedophiles who do
the right thing only because it is the right
thing to do and don't give a fuck about society
and its goddamn rules and I think Jesus
would have broken bread
with me and my friends.

And my friends
love me
because I am like them
and I love them
because they are like me

And some days
they are all I have
and some days
I am all they've got

And together
we are a family
and together
we can hold on
to the tiny thread
that keeps us sane as we watch
the people around us pour their friendship down the drain
like so much cold shitty coffee at the after church social
hour.

To Tell

I want to tell her:
her brown eyes light
the room,
the dark,
my heart

I want to tell her:
her hair is
stranded in lovely,
purposely careless,
uncensored amazing.

I want to tell her:
I was lost before her,
her voice sings softly to the dark of me.
That I cannot imagine
without her,
without me.

But I don't because:

Men can't

talk to

friends

like

that.

Sylvia

You, you, you
are gone. Two kids and
family behind, I read your words
where have you been?

Broken girl, did
Daddy help? He did me
broke me, took me
shot me, threw me
down, down, down.

We must go to town,
to see you, hear the sound
the blue wave, hiss, hiss
it says. The oven, hiss
hiss hisses loud.

Your words make me
what I am. What am I?
What were you? How did
you get to leave? Easy way
out. Fuckin cheater.

I don't get it, your
choice, life, death,
I only understand your
words, broken, empty,
pain. I feel it too.

A talent. Who
fucking cares? Hissing
at the back door. Snakes
in the woodpile. Where is
Daddy now?

Can you tell? Can you tell, in
heaven, or in hell? Or
was that just here? Where
the pain is. Where
I am still.

Sylvia, you are my
Teacher, Mother, Sister,
Curse. And what we come to?
decisions, decisions, decisions
snakes at the door, hiss, hiss.

I did it, why couldn't
you? I'm doing it, why
can't you? You did it, why
can't I? Snakes at the back
door. Hiss, hiss, hiss.

"Greater love has no one than this, that he lay down his life for his friends,"

which is probably why I have so few

I do not come to paper with pen lightly.

Remember, my friend: I

told you

warned you

as all writers should

before...

"The Beauty of 'Fuck'"

The word slips off my

tongue

like air, water.

And Mrs. H--

"Why do you use that word?"

she is offended and informs me that

"It's an ugly word to describe something beautiful."

but to me it's

"just a word?"

"Yes."

So she changes the channel to a show

on MTV about a teenager with a giant cock, who

rubs his ballsweat on another young man's

nose

and she starts to laugh

"This is funny?"

She giggles, "yes!"

"But 'fuck' is offensive?"

"Yes."

I have heard her say
"Men..."
The way my father said
"Cunts..."
and when I try to compliment her
her children, her husband
she tells me
"You have to say that
because you're my friend."

She reads 50 Shades
and
shows me a picture of
Channing Tatum's chest
asking
"Could there be a more perfect man?"
"I dunno, when I watch porn,
I just call it porn."

"No one had sex
and they weren't naked
in that movie."
as she objectifies
another human being
into nothing more than a fuckable toy.

But it's okay
he's just a
"Men..."

and I don't
argue because
I call her "friend"
and these days I'm glad to have friends
who are blessed enough to not have to know
why I have to call things
what they are.

Self

Dr. Angelou,

I hope you will forgive the intrusion. I hope you will understand the need. Most of all, I hope you will know that I have to say things as they are; because although differently, I too am:

Caged

I know why the caged bird sings
because it cannot cry

I know why the caged bird sings
because it cannot fly

I know why the caged bird sings
because it is a bird
and that's what birds do

I know why the caged bird sings
because it is un-flocked

I know why the caged bird sings
because it is a bird
caged

I know why the caged bird sings
because I am
and I do.

How to Write Poetry

Dear Sir or Madam,

I have heard that you wish to know how to write poetry and that you do not know how. As you have asked me for instructions and I am a poet, I will attempt to give you the best that I know of how to write what you must come to call poetry. I hope that these words will be sufficient for you, as they are honestly all I know about writing.

I am assuming that you have made a habit out of reading poetry. If you have not, start. Read the masters: Poe, Yeats, Thoreau, Plath, Whitman, Olson, and anyone else that you find calls to the very nature of who you are.

And once you have read them, ignore their rules, syntax, diction, and force yourself to speak your own voice. Your voice is you at your worst, yelling at your children, throwing rocks at cars, and laughing at elderly women as they fall and break their hips. Get comfortable with it, embrace it, hold that miscreant dear, and do not be ashamed or embarrassed by what others may judge you for. They will judge you, and when they do, pull your bastard inner child out and tell 'em to fuck off in the most polite and socially acceptable way possible.

Tell the truth and lie only when necessary to make the truth more evident. And when you lie, be proud of it.

Tell your friends and family that your skeletons are coming out. Some of them will leave. Let them.

Get comfortable with using profanity, as every motherfucking nigger bitch-ass cunt should, and only use it when necessary. They are words, words are your tools, and nothing is sacred. Even God is a fucking whore sometimes. Kneel before your words. Humbleness is better than righteousness. Unless righteousness is needed, then refer to the comment about lying.

And finally, write... about everything. Shamelessly. Bleed your pain onto paper, embarrass your friends and family, let your secret loves escape, and apologize for nothing, not one word.

Sincerely,

Michael Barry

Swimming Lessons

       5

Swimming lessons at dads,

flung into the Blue River.

Water enveloping my body,

my mouth, my nose.

Rocks at my back,

the bottom, safety.

I stand from the water afraid,

father laughing above.

       7

Swimming lessons at the YMCA,

at the pool, not

Blue River.

Final swim test in clothes: shirt,

Levi 501's, shoes.

Fifteen minutes treading water

no sweat.

10

The ocean: Mighty Pacific, a riptide.

My family swims chest deep,

Ankles snatched and

salty water forces

into nose

out of mouth

gurgling water speeding past

my feet hit something hard.

I bob to the top.

Salty water on lips,

leaking from eyes.

His family 100 yards away,

he swims to them, an angle to shore.

18

The Snake, through Hell's Canyon:

they weren't fucking joking.

The water class 5 and:

"No women on this boat."

"Who are the best swimmers?"

"Who has whitewater experience?"

"What rivers?"

Overinflate the boat.

The guide makes me ride in back,

to help him steer.

No one knows how to drive and our boat is

a drunken spider meandering towards the first set.

The man next to me falls out, clings to the raft

his terrified eyes beg me, I hit him in the chest with my paddle,

save his life and he hates me for it.

Two thumbs up from the guide.

First set looks like a ripple,

and another fifteen feet out.

We approach:

the guide laughs at the men in front,

running to the back of the boat,

like that'll help. Fucking idiots, my best friend

among them. I can see it now. A fifteen foot bowl,

the mouth of the rapid, eager, hungry, growling

it swallows the raft,

flexes its jaws and folds the boat in half.

Suddenly I am airborne, an unintended human missile

above the water, laughing.

Catch the eye of my best friend,

his fear equals my joy.

To "Bud"

A woman recently told
me that "Men
can't be raped."

But you and I know
different.

A swinging light in
your basement, the pachinko
balls ring, and we know what fits
into the places where it shouldn't. Tearing
apart the small things of little boys.

Sometimes that wound still
bleeds, and every time I take a shit, I am trying to push you
out of me

I do not remember what I told the judge, I just pull
open the brass handled courtroom door
and I am back on the hallway carpet again
blinking, with the middle gone
like so many middles with you.

Broken,

split

am I and this is what we parts have to say:

Your prison was nowhere near as long as mine

If you are done fucking children, Do
Not Tell.
Because I can
forgive but
I cannot
forget the four years I
cannot remember.

If you are not, Do
Not Tell.
Because what you
and my family
created
in me
will make me to sleep and come for you, to growl low in
your ear and find what cannot fit in you but will.

You will do this for me

for I do not think

I can take

another break-

ing. And your silence

will last

longer than

mine.

Texting

Typing words through
A T-9 interface with the option of a QWERTY pad
To tell my friend that I care
To warn her, and for that
I am called and asshole; sexist
For the third time.
She won't apologize, I won't put up with it, and she doesn't understand why we aren't talking anymore. And now it's TWO friends down in less than six months and that's gotta be a fuckin record.

Facebook, Myspace, Texting, Twitter.

People are more connected now than they have ever been
And yet our connection,
Is lost.
Broken phrased and acronymed to death
Our words are empty and hollow.
While we hunger so much for the intimacy promised to us on every Hallmark card that somehow people have come to believe that they DO have 896 friends.

But how many of those motherfuckers gonna help you move?
How many will again...
While these lies of "friendship" have people speaking things they do not mean and the knee jerk reactions have become something that is accepted by all those who are "Connected"
Or not.

I kill my Facebook account on average five times per year.
And the only reason I have kept it at all is because...

I am lonely.
Seeking understanding in a world that does not value the things I value most,
Love,
Kindness
Hope,
Words.

That connect a lonely soldier from the empty desert to his family by way of a letter and a stamp.
Words that are chosen carefully because the message being sent is on a five-day delay and HE KNOWS that when that letter is read he may not even be alive.
Except in words.
The soldier knows the pen IS mightier than the sword, but it can't do shit against the send button that you murder your friend with from your living room.

So please, be careful with your words.
And remember the beauty of our eyes when you speak.

Because if you can't stand to see what your words are doing, then maybe you should stop scribbling alone in the dark.

To-Day

Today, I ate
picked the gravel
from the meat

Today, I spoke
and no one heard me

Today, I
woke up

Today, I
laid down

Today, I
listened to music

Today, I
lost all faith in humanity

Today, I
decided I'd rather be dead than alone and
today, my dog saved my fuckin life.

Today, I
woke up

Today, I
am tired

Today, I
lost a friend

Today, I
prefer the gun to hunger

Today, I
couldn't pray

Today, I am alone

Today, I am alone

Today, I am alone
again.

Ages

I was never two years old.
Handcuffed to the bed
to my brother, to lay
still when we nap.

I was never four or five either.
Watched Dad put his
wedding ring on the table
on top of words I could not read.
"I'm sorry, son."
And then I'm dragging my father to bed
with a needle in his arm
Jake was shot
I was
raped
the switch
stung
a cigar put out on my arm
and "If you lose a fight
you can't come home."
I broke his nose, I won.
Split the wood, light the fire

sharpen the knife, roll the cigarettes
cook the breakfast, do the homework
oil the boots, and...
I ran out of time for four, five, six, and seven.

Nine
I never was.
Smoking pot, attempting suicide
my first hallucinogen
selling drugs, punched my teacher
school suspensions, hid from Mom
lost my best friend
tried to kill my uncle
quit counting fights, killed the
neighbor's dog for attacking my cat
new shoes, old jeans
and I'm just gettin' started.

12
don't know that either.
Lost weeks in my mind
insomnia
meth helps, selling more
caring less
lost, gone.
And I wrote my first poem

16
finally not.
Clean for one year, sobriety
sucks, hypnotherapy, a broken
mind, confusion
tears finally, I begin to date
my first wife, writing often.
Alternative school, probation, therapy
strong dissociative disorder...
Y'know, 16.

23

Married for three years, disabled
for five, and finally an accurate
diagnosis. PTSD and more
therapy, pills that work
coping skills, meditation
breathe deep, relax
write.

30

Divorced, sober, working
off meds, writing and
raising my brother's son.

35

Homeless, divorce #2, associates degree
writing, working and
finally beginning to see
I have no concept of family
I have no sense of community
I have never had parents
I have no Idea what it means to be 23
let alone how to
act my age.

Country

American Real

Wally and the Beav were a lie.
And the Brady's
I don't think existed
anywhere
but in the mind's eye of some
over-paid writer who
wanted to sell us
Bullshit America.

In my America
children are beaten with boards
until both the child and the board
are broken
and the splinters are all that is left
to be picked out of each other.

In my America
children are raped
and their mothers send them back for more.

In my America
Children are made to brush their teeth
with their fingers
and baking soda
because they are poor
and even though their mothers
work three fucking jobs
all they can afford to eat is peanut butter
and milk
and that,
not always.

In my America
Pain is carried under the skin
from so many years
of abuse that the touch of another person
is excruciating and is always
avoided
which makes holding hands
a big fucking deal.

In my America

Dogs help us sleep

let us know when there's danger

and they are the only living thing we can touch

that doesn't hurt.

In my America

we learn to fight before write

murder before love

kill before calm

and there's no sense of place for me in my America.

In my America

you learn to roll a joint at 5

smoke one by 8

sell one by 9

and are tryin to stop at 15.

In my America

I believe in Jesus

not because I know he loves me

or the church is good

but because I had to learn right and wrong from somewhere

for fuck's sake
it wasn't comin' from home.

And in my America
when we learn right
we do right
and we don't fucking lie
not even about the Cleavers
or the Brady's when it comes to
my America.

Antoinette America

And our soldiers died for this.
Thirty percent tax
when God only asks for ten,
3-D television
so we can experience plastic reality,
a microwave
to destroy our food

fuck that.

Our buildings
destroyed
and we raid oil
fields. Our people
sick
and we are told
to buy
insurance.

"Let them eat cake."

Thank you,
> Mr. Obama
> Mr. Bush
> Mr. Clinton

thank you all very much. Now get the fuck out.

Here's what I know:
Democracy is mob
rule
and if you control
the mob you control the rule
America was a republic.
You want more $$$$$$$?
come get it.

You have lied
to us for too long
and one more tax
and...

Not all of us are asleep

Not all of us are stupid

Not all of us will lay down

and We

Awake

are not

as afraid

as you

think.

Push

it much farther

and we'll see

if Jefferson

was right

when he said,

"The tree of liberty must be refreshed from time to time with the blood of patriots and tyrants."

Matters of Importance

Words Unspoken

My mother was raped
by her father
and her father
learned that from his.
It was not bred
not born
but it was learned
survived
In Words Unspoken.

When my mother sent me
to the man who raped me
against my will
for four years
In Words Unspoken.

When my father broke
a board on my ass
a cigar on my arm
I drug him to bed
unconscious, heroin
In Words Unspoken.

I learned wrong
In Words Unspoken
hurt people
In Words Unspoken
mind broken
In Words Unspoken

people are raped
In Words Unspoken
murdered
In Words Unspoken
molested
In Words Unspoken
beaten
In Words Unspoken
broken
In Words Unspoken
starved
In Words Unspoken
and no weapon on earth can kill more
than Words Unspoken.

I was mute until I was 15.

my mother had her tongue stitched on at 50.

my father, no mouth

my brother, choked shut

I won't know the day they die

I'm losing my father

to Words Unspoken

my brother

to Words Unspoken

aunts, uncles, grandparents, cousins, two wives, my childhood

to Words Unspoken

And all I can do,

is speak.

Made in the USA
Charleston, SC
18 March 2013